Spooky HOUSE

By Carol Krueger
Illustrated by Richard Hoit

spooky HOUSE

Predict: What will the problem be?

Ashlee would never forget the first time she saw the old house. It was very old and the paint had become dirty white flakes. The roof was a rusty red. Most of the windows were cracked and a creeper crawled right up to the crooked chimney. The inside of the house smelt mouldy and musty and there seemed to be a spider in every corner.

"I can't live in this house!" thought Ashlee.

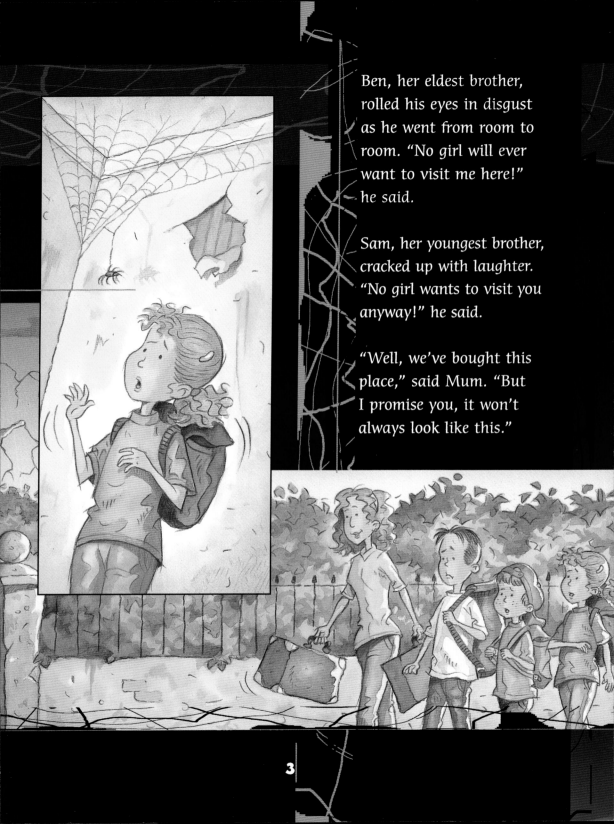

Ben, her eldest brother, rolled his eyes in disgust as he went from room to room. "No girl will ever want to visit me here!" he said.

Sam, her youngest brother, cracked up with laughter. "No girl wants to visit you anyway!" he said.

"Well, we've bought this place," said Mum. "But I promise you, it won't always look like this."

By lunchtime a furniture van had pulled up outside. Two men started carrying things up the path. Ashlee opened the door.

"Have we got the right house?" one of them asked. "This is the delivery for the Parker family."

Mum nodded. "Yes, this is the right address."

The man gave her a strange look. "This place has been for sale for years, ever since that crazy old scientist died," he said. "Strange things happen here!"

Sam's eyes opened wide. "What sort of things?"

"Weird noises and eerie lights," said the man. "If I were you, I wouldn't ever go near the attic."

Mum interrupted. "Those are just stories. We're going to turn this place into a great home!"

.

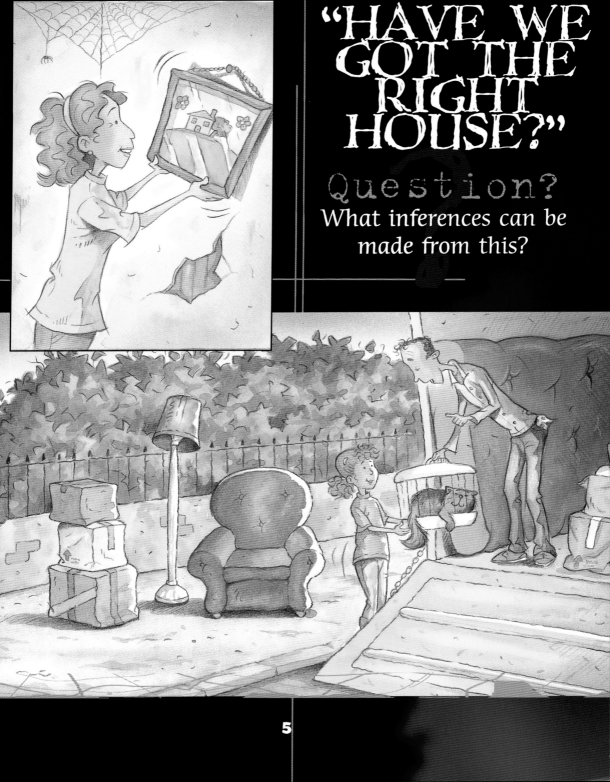

"HAVE WE GOT THE RIGHT HOUSE?"

Question?

What inferences can be made from this?

The men carried in the furniture and dozens of boxes. Ashlee took some things to her room. The window looked out over a huge tree. It seemed twisted and gnarled – like the house. The wallpaper had turned yellow and one piece curled down from the ceiling like a large banana peel. Ashlee felt like crying.

LIKE A LARGE BANANA PEEL

Metaphor or Simile?

A `simile` creates a mind picture in which one thing is said to be like another. The word *like* or *as* is used to make the comparison.

A `metaphor` creates a mind picture in which one thing is described as if it were actually that thing.

Throughout the night Ashlee lay in her bed listening for strange sounds. The only thing that made her feel better was Sharkey. He lay curled up on the end of her bed. He purred, but he had one ear turned back apprehensively – just to make sure that he didn't miss anything in this new strange place.

Question?

Why do you think Ashlee felt better about things because of Sharkey's presence?

A   uneasily

B   contentedly

C   ready

At school, everybody teased Ashlee and Sam about moving into the old house.

"That's a weird house!" they all said. "It's old and eerie."

Ashlee was glad when her new friend Rachel came over after school. Ashlee showed her around the house. "This is actually a cool house!" said Rachel. "It's a shame about all those stories."

"What stories?" Ashlee asked nervously.

"Well – a really strange scientist used to live here. There were always odd things happening," said Rachel.

"Like what?" asked Ashlee.

"People said that they saw weird lights in the house, which illuminated the whole sky, and Mrs Cole at number 18 said coloured smoke curled out of the chimney."

"But the scientist hasn't lived here for ages," protested Ashlee. She felt suddenly cold as if she had been plunged into an icy whirlpool. She changed the subject: "Let's go and see what Sam's up to."

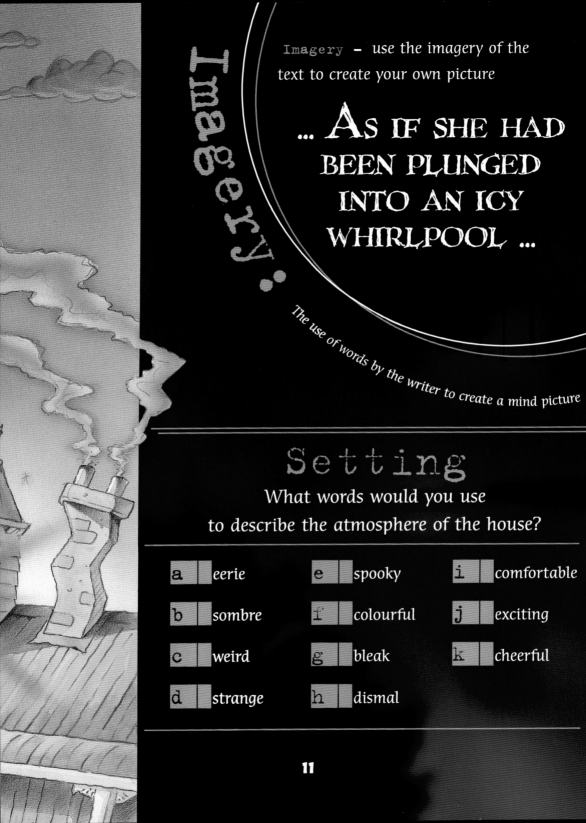

Imagery – use the imagery of the text to create your own picture

... AS IF SHE HAD BEEN PLUNGED INTO AN ICY WHIRLPOOL ...

The use of words by the writer to create a mind picture

Setting

What words would you use to describe the atmosphere of the house?

a	eerie	e	spooky	i	comfortable
b	sombre	f	colourful	j	exciting
c	weird	g	bleak	k	cheerful
d	strange	h	dismal		

Ashlee knocked on Sam's door.

"No password – no entry!" Sam shouted back.

Ashlee groaned and then she remembered. "Sharkey!"

The door opened. Sam and his mate Yee were at the computer. Yee grinned at them. "I can't believe that I'm actually sitting inside this old house!" he said. "No one ever dared to come here! Even Hero Boy and his mates run like frightened hares past the gate."

Ashlee felt a bit nauseous. She turned away but Ben was blocking the doorway. "Guess what?" he said. "I've got a job after school in the chocolate factory! I start tomorrow."

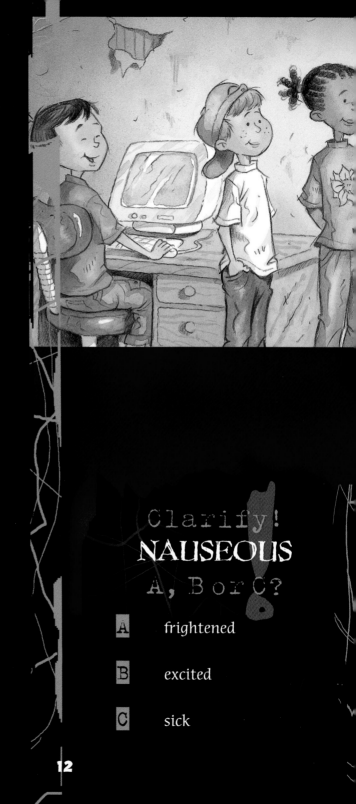

Clarify!
NAUSEOUS
A, B or C?

A   frightened

B   excited

C   sick

"I wish I was old enough to work there," said Rachel. "It's boring just hanging about." Then she smiled slowly. "Hey, why don't we go and check out the attic! That would impress Hero Boy and his . . ."

"We're not going up there!" said Sam.

"Maybe it's not such a good idea," said Ashlee.

"Well I'm not scared," said Ben. "I'll go there by myself."

Question?

Why do you think Ashlee said "Maybe it's not such a good idea."?

Everyone tried to talk him out of it, but Ben went up the stairs. The others waited in Sam's room in frozen silence. There were no screams, no noises, and after a while Ben came back.

"Well????" everyone said.

"It's locked," said Ben. "No one can get in."

Question?
What is meant by the term *frozen silence*?

Before long the old house started to look and smell better. It had new carpet and pale lemon walls. The front of the house had been painted white and the chimney was straight. Mum had planted rows of roses that marched like prickly soldiers along the path. "I think people will start calling this 'the grand house' now," she said proudly.

Ashlee felt better about her new home. Now she felt fine about asking her friends for a sleepover.

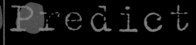

Predict:

What could happen in this story now? Has the problem been resolved?

Personification:
The likening of human characteristics to things and ideas

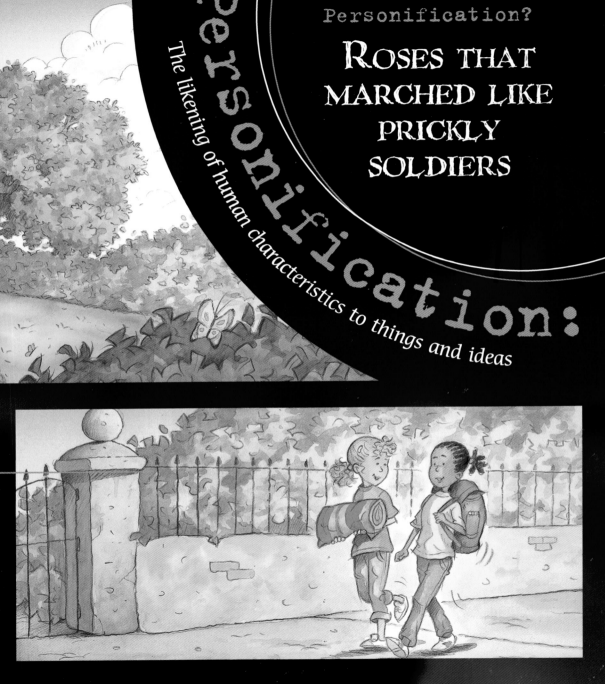

Is this Personification?

ROSES THAT MARCHED LIKE PRICKLY SOLDIERS

On Friday night, Rachel came over to stay. But at midnight Ashlee woke up with a start. She froze, beads of perspiration running down her forehead. Something was moving in the attic. She listened anxiously. Rachel sat bolt upright in the bed next to her, her face white with fear. "There's something there!" she whispered.

Sharkey growled and looked up in the direction of the attic above with staring eyes that glowed like glass beads. His ears flattened against his head and his fur was fluffed in fright.

Ashlee pulled the blankets over her head and heard Rachel do the same. Her heart thumped. There was something in the attic. Something strange and fearful. Something that could not be explained. She wondered as the night travelled on to day if she would ever get used to living there.

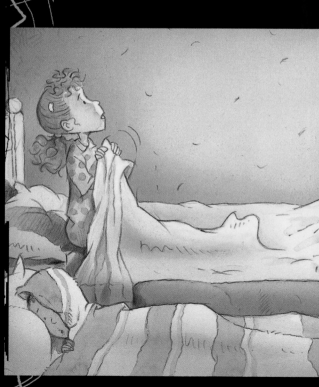

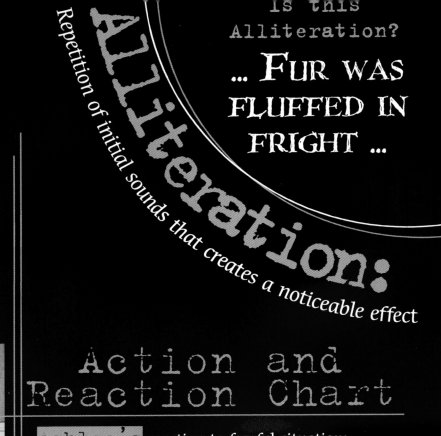

Is this Alliteration?

... **FUR WAS FLUFFED IN FRIGHT** ...

Alliteration:
Repetition of initial sounds that creates a noticeable effect

Action and Reaction Chart

Ashlee's reaction to fearful situation:

There was something in the attic - something strange and fearful

➡

She pulled the blankets over her head

Her heart thumped.

Sharkey's reaction to fearful situation:

There was something in the attic - something strange and fearful

➡

In the morning, Ice came to visit. He knocked loudly on the front door. "I saw a light in the attic last night!" he cried. "It was creepy! Why don't we do an investigation to find out what's up there?" he said. "You know, like they do on TV."

Ashlee fought back the fears of the night. "You're right. Let's do it!"

"Awesome!" said Sam.

"You won't find anything," said Ben. "Creepy houses exist only in the celluloid world!"

Question?
What does the term celluloid world mean?

"You're right. Let's do it!"

Question?
Why do you think
Ashlee had to fight back
the fears of the night?

Sam, Yee, Rachel and Ashlee spent the rest of the morning investigating the history of the house, with Ben, yapping like a terrier after a rat, behind them. Sam and Rachel first interviewed Mrs Cole at number 18, who said that she had seen the lights twice that week. Ashlee and Yee went to the library and found that the name of the scientist who had owned the house was Alfred Wordsworth. They looked him up in the scientific journals. She discovered he had been well known for his scientific theories on the reactions of chemical combinations forged by heat. She also discovered that the attic had been his laboratory.

We need to see what is going on up there," said Yee. "We have to open the attic."

"Mum will have a key," said Ashlee.

YAPPING LIKE A TERRIER AFTER A RAT

Metaphor or Simile?

Check back to page 7

Clarify!
THEORY
A, B or C?

A   plans

B   ideas that explore and explain

C   understandings

But Mum didn't have a key. "I don't know why the key was not with the other house keys," said Mum.

She rang all the locksmiths in town but no one would come. "We've heard too many stories about that attic!" they said. "We would need danger money to open that door!"

Mum went upstairs, and everybody followed. Ashlee's heart was pounding in her chest. She could hear it pounding, pounding, pounding like bongo drums in her chest. She held Sharkey so tightly that his claws dug into her skin.

Mum grabbed the handle and shouldered the door. "The door's not locked!" Mum whispered.

Question?
What is meant by the term danger money?

Slowly Mum pushed the door of the attic open. Then she gasped. There was a strange silence. "Come and look!" she called.

Everyone crowded into the attic. The room was bare but there, in the middle of the floor, was Ben . . . surrounded with bags of chocolates. His mouth was full and his face was as red as a strawberry. Beside him lay a large torch and the cast-off wrappers of chocolates.

"Well – what are you all staring at? I reckoned this was a good place to keep the chocolates I was allowed to bring home from work. I knew they'd be safe from you chocoholics!" Then he grinned. "Would you all like some?"

Character profiles

 Mum strong, independent, confident, calm

 Ashlee **?**

 Ben **?**

 Sam excitable, enthusiastic, mischievous, forthright

Key elements of the story

a Family moved to a new home

b They were scared by stories about strange and mysterious happenings at the house

c Mum planted roses

d Ben got a job in a chocolate factory

e Sam and Yee played on the computer

f The children decided to investigate the happenings and get to the bottom of the stories

g They found there was no truth in the stories

WHICH ARE THE KEY POINTS YOU WOULD INCLUDE IN A SUMMARY OF THIS STORY?

Think about the text

What connections can you make
to the emotions, situations or
characters of *Spooky House*?

Text to Student

EMBARRASSMENT

DETERMINATION

APPREHENSION

RELIEF

NERVOUSNESS

UPSET

ANXIETY

INSECURITY

FEAR

CURIOSITY

BEING TEASED

FAMILY RIVALRY

MOVING TO A NEW HOME

SINGLE-PARENT FAMILY

BELIEVING A RUMOUR

TEXT TO TEXT

Talk about other stories you may have read that have similar features. Compare the stories.

TEXT TO WORLD

Talk about situations in the world that might connect to elements in the story.

Planning a Mystery

DECIDE ON A STRANGE EVENT OR HAPPENING

Strange lights in an old house

DECIDE ON THE CHARACTERS

THINK ABOUT THE WAY A CHARACTER WILL THINK, ACT AND FEEL.

Ashlee   Mum   Ben   Sam

Yee and Rachel

DECIDE ON SETTING

Setting

- LOCATION
- TIME
- ATMOSPHERE

DECIDE ON THE EVENTS THAT BUILD THE SUSPENSE

DECIDE ON HOW THE MYSTERY WILL BE SOLVED.

IS THERE A SURPRISE ENDING? WILL THERE BE AN

UNEXPECTED TWIST?

Mystery Stories Can...

a Have a surprise that misleads the reader

b Have clues that help solve the mystery

c Record responses from characters that depict fear, apprehension, alarm, bravery ...

d Evoke uneasiness in the reader through imagery and setting